HOW TO SET UP A VENTURE CAPITAL FUND

A Quick Start Guide to Launching Your VC Fund Right Now and Preparing for Institutional Scale and Success

Winter Mead

First Edition

How To Set Up a Venture Capital Fund

Copyright © 2024 by Winter Mead.

All rights reserved. No part of this publication may be reproduced, distributed or transmitted in any form or by any means, including photocopying, recording, or other electronic or mechanical methods, without the prior written permission of the publisher, except in the case of brief quotations embodied in critical reviews and certain other noncommercial uses permitted by copyright law.

Winter Mead, San Francisco, CA

How To Set Up a Venture Capital Fund / Winter Mead. —1st ed.

Trade Paperback: 979-8-9907726-8-7

Hardcover: 979-8-9907726-9-4

Audiobook: 979-8-9907726-1-8

eBook: 979-8-9907726-2-5

To my family, in particular Danesha and Jude,
who've supported another effort on the writing front

Contents

WHY I WROTE THIS BOOK 1

DEFINITIONS 5

    WHAT IS VENTURE CAPITAL? 5

    WHAT IS A VENTURE CAPITALIST? 5

    WHAT IS A VENTURE CAPITAL FUND? 6

    WHAT IS A VENTURE CAPITAL FIRM? 6

    WHAT IS THE DIFFERENCE BETWEEN A VENTURE CAPITAL FUND AND A VENTURE CAPITAL FIRM? 7

INTRODUCTION: WHAT IS THE SCOPE OF THIS BOOK? 9

    SETTING UP A FUND AND KNOWING WHO IS RESPONSIBLE FOR SETTING UP THE STEPS, RANKING THE IMPORTANCE OF EACH STEP, AND THE PERSPECTIVES BEHIND THEM 9

        WHAT IS INVOLVED IN SETTING UP A FUND? 10

        WHO IS RESPONSIBLE FOR SETTING UP THE VENTURE CAPITAL FUND? 10

STEPS IN SETTING UP A VENTURE CAPITAL FUND 11

RANKING THE IMPORTANCE OF EACH STEP IN SETTING UP A VENTURE CAPITAL FUND 12

PERSPECTIVES ON SETTING UP A VENTURE CAPITAL FUND 13

TWO MAIN PERSPECTIVES: THE VENTURE CAPITALIST AND THE LIMITED PARTNER .. 13

THE FRAMEWORK OF THIS BOOK 15

UNDERSTAND THE THREE PHASES OF SETTING UP A VC FUND, THE CORE FUNCTIONAL AREAS NEEDED, AND HOW THEY ALL FIT TOGETHER 15

THE THREE PHASES OF SETTING UP A VC FUND 15

THE CORE FUNCTIONAL AREAS COVERED IN THIS BOOK... 16

HOW DO THE CORE FUNCTIONAL AREAS FIT INTO THE THREE PHASES OF SETTING UP A VC FUND 17

PHASE 1: SETTING UP THE BASIC FUNCTIONS REQUIRED FOR YOUR VENTURE CAPITAL FIRM 23

    UNIT 0. BASIC LEGAL, BANKING, AND FINANCE 24

    UNIT 1. CLOUD PROVIDER 25

    UNIT 2. TELECOMMUNICATIONS 29

    UNIT 3. THE CUSTOMER RELATIONSHIP MANAGEMENT SYSTEM 33

    LEARN WHAT GOES INTO CREATING A VERY GOOD CRM SYSTEM AND HOW TO BEST USE IT TO YOUR ADVANTAGE 33

    UNIT 4. INVESTOR RELATIONS: MARKETING AND SALES 38

PHASE 2: SETTING UP THE BASIC FUNCTIONS OF YOUR VENTURE CAPITAL FUND 45

    BASIC FUNCTIONS OF YOUR VC FUND AND THE CORE SERVICE PROVIDERS NEEDED TO RUN IT 45

    UNIT 5. LEGAL CONSIDERATIONS RELATED TO A VC FIRM 46

UNIT 6. THE WHO, WHAT, WHY, WHEN, AND HOW OF VC FUNDS AND BANKING..............56

UNIT 7. FUND ADMINISTRATION AND ITS PURPOSE 62

UNIT 8. THE IMPORTANCE OF THE TAX FUNCTION 67

PHASE 3: ADDITIONAL FUNCTIONS THAT SUPPORT GROWTH TO BECOMING AN INSTITUTIONAL FIRM 75

UNIT 9. FUNCTIONS EXPECTED BY INSTITUTIONAL LIMITED PARTNERS, INCLUDING THE AUDIT 75

UNIT 10. OTHER CONSIDERATIONS WHEN SETTING UP YOUR VENTURE CAPITAL FUND 86

COMPENDIUM: KEY TAKE-AWAYS................... 95

EPILOGUE: WHAT THIS BOOK IS… AND WHAT IT IS NOT 97

ABOUT THE AUTHOR 99

WHY I WROTE THIS BOOK

In 2021 I published the book *How To Raise a Venture Capital Fund*, which serves as a guide to venture capitalists (VCs) to help them understand how to raise money from their investors, called Limited Partners (LPs). Afterwards, having spoken with hundreds of VCs who read it and were actively building funds of their own, I noted a key knowledge gap: many VCs are still struggling with how to set up their VC firms the right way from Day 0.

Even as software now allows entrepreneurs to independently manage a fund, and specialized service providers are available to support these operations, a gap still exists in understanding how to set up a fund properly. This includes seeing the big picture, identifying the various functions required for a fund and when to build them, and understanding who, ultimately, should be responsible for these functions. This process can take months or even years to understand, time that could be better spent building your firm.

This book is for venture capitalists looking for the information they need to move faster and more efficiently in growing their VC firm.

While there are many books on how to invest, there are actually very few that directly address how to set up a venture capital fund. One of the most difficult stages of any business is getting it off the ground. Since 2011, I have invested in over 100 VC funds and have launched another 150 VC funds through my company, Coolwater. This book gives you the tools to set up a venture capital fund properly from the start. I take you step by step through every part of the process, saving you all the time that would otherwise be spent (aka wasted) on puzzling out what you don't know or in defining an operational plan from scratch.

Setting your fund up the right way also means less risk for your Limited Partners. For those new to the VC world, LPs are the wealthy individuals or institutions that invest in a VC fund with the expectation that the fund will deliver a certain multiple of return. For example, an LP might expect that $1 invested in the fund today will return $3 a decade from now. If you think about these numbers in the millions, tens of millions, or hundreds of millions, you see that a VC can play a large role in wealth creation over a relatively short period of time.

This book will help you optimize for success by avoiding costly mistakes such as never getting your fund off the ground in the first place because you're always fighting fires on the operational side or not optimizing for investing and fundraising. *How To Set Up A Venture Capital Fund* offers a way to increase your probability of success in launching your VC fund.

This book additionally focuses on the importance of innovation. Innovation at scale requires financing, and VC firms finance a large part of today's innovations. I've witnessed first-hand how venture capital influences most of our everyday lives. Early-stage VC firms are the first believers and investors in future technology.

This book not only offers a practical approach to helping you set up a venture capital firm, but it was also designed to help you move towards your goals more efficiently and with less stress. In short, my intent is to simplify your journey while making it more fulfilling and more productive. You are starting out as a first-time VC fund manager with the objective of attracting investors to finance innovation, and I want that effort to be rewarding for you.

Think of it this way: the goal – your goal – should be *setting up the machine* that is your VC fund. You want your business to run smoothly, with all the right systems and processes. By actively considering how the systems you are building will allow you to scale, you give yourself more time to spend on investing, fundraising, and enhancing your portfolio companies.

DEFINITIONS

As we dive in, let's review some terminology around venture capital to be clear what it is (and isn't), who a venture capitalist is, and the key differences between a VC fund and a VC firm.

WHAT IS VENTURE CAPITAL?

As David Swensen defines it in his seminal book *Pioneering Portfolio Management*, venture capital is a type of private equity "providing financing and company building skills to start-up operations with the goal of developing companies into substantial, profitable enterprises." Venture capital is uniquely intended to help support businesses at the beginning of their development.

WHAT IS A VENTURE CAPITALIST?

Venture capitalists are the investors who provide financing to start-ups in exchange for an equity stake (or ownership share) in the business.

WHAT IS A VENTURE CAPITAL FUND?

Venture capitalists manage venture capital funds, the pool of money that will be invested. Think of these funds as small businesses that are set up for the sole purpose of investing in promising start-ups.

WHAT IS A VENTURE CAPITAL FIRM?

When you start your own venture capital fund, you are responsible for more than just investing in start-ups. In fact, you become the manager of your own business, called the venture capital firm. Just as in running any small business, you are responsible for all of the functions of that business. You are essentially assuming the role of Chief Executive Officer (CEO). You will have to set up and manage your business and deal with problems as they arise to keep your firm running. I'll use this CEO analogy throughout this book because while you may be solely responsible when first setting up your venture capital firm, you soon will begin to hire and delegate responsibilities to others as you grow, just as any CEO does in scaling their business.

WHAT IS THE DIFFERENCE BETWEEN A VENTURE CAPITAL FUND AND A VENTURE CAPITAL FIRM?

It is important to understand the difference between the venture capital fund – the pool of money that is used to invest in young companies – and the venture capital firm, the operating business that manages everything else, such as paying rent, paying yourself, hiring employees, managing data, and (hopefully) raising additional venture capital funds.

You are reading this book because, presumably, you want to raise a venture capital fund. However, keep in mind that if you are successful in establishing a fund, then you will ultimately also be running an operating business, often called the management company. The focus of this book is to describe each step in the process of successfully raising your first venture capital fund. As you grow and add additional funds, your firm will become more complex.

INTRODUCTION: WHAT IS THE SCOPE OF THIS BOOK?

SETTING UP A FUND AND KNOWING WHO IS RESPONSIBLE FOR SETTING UP THE STEPS, RANKING THE IMPORTANCE OF EACH STEP, AND THE PERSPECTIVES BEHIND THEM

Readers of this book are interested in understanding how to set up a business to manage venture capital funds. This book lays out how to spend less time figuring out how to set up a venture capital firm so you can start off with a strong foundation for a firm that can eventually scale.

WHAT IS INVOLVED IN SETTING UP A FUND?

Setting up a VC fund is setting up a small business. There are always necessary steps when launching any business, and this is no different in the sense that it is a process. However, there are particular nuances to setting up a venture capital fund. We will review what systems and processes should be put in place to launch a venture capital fund and what third-party service providers and software tools you will need to engage and use properly to ensure your fund's success.

WHO IS RESPONSIBLE FOR SETTING UP THE VENTURE CAPITAL FUND?

You are responsible for setting up your fund. And this book is written for you as the manager of this launch process. Eventually someone else may take over this operational role, but in the beginning, it is your time, dedication, and organization that will make it work.

STEPS IN SETTING UP A VENTURE CAPITAL FUND

There is an order of operations for setting up a fund. This is based on when you will need to set up the operations to build a reputable firm and launch a lucrative fund. The steps should build upon each other, but note that there can be different ways to order these steps in real-world practice.

There may be third-party service providers, for example, that could combine several functions and offer you a "one-size-fits-all" solution. If you choose to work with a service provider that offers, for example, legal, fund administration, and tax support, it is wise to understand how these functions are set up, so you are in a better position to manage these areas of your firm and handle any concerns that may arise. There may be a point, for instance, when you may still temporarily need to step into a negotiating role for the legal function, or an accounting role for fund administration, or a decision-making role for tax purposes. It is to your advantage to know how all of the pieces fit together. A greater perspective means well-informed decisions for your venture capital business.

RANKING THE IMPORTANCE OF EACH STEP IN SETTING UP A VENTURE CAPITAL FUND

In this book, I offer my opinions and recommendations for setting up a fund. Each of the steps discussed below will improve your business processes and ultimately save time and effort so you can focus on what is most important as an investor: investing, fundraising, and adding value to your portfolio. Consider that each of the recommended steps has an associated cost, and that therefore there are trade-offs on a case-by-case basis. I attempt to keep the steps as simple and as objective as possible, while offering you as much perspective as possible to encourage better decision-making for your venture capital business.

Some steps may be more or less relevant because there can be many types of investors and even different types of funds within venture capital investing. As these nuances arise, I will attempt to provide perspective on how to think about these different circumstances.

PERSPECTIVES ON SETTING UP A VENTURE CAPITAL FUND

TWO MAIN PERSPECTIVES: THE VENTURE CAPITALIST AND THE LIMITED PARTNER

For the VC perspective, I take an operator perspective, which helps to "cut through the noise" and help you understand what actually needs to be set up. The VC perspective shares what is most important in terms of function, cost, and effectiveness. As a VC operator, you will want to set up an efficient, effective, and productive business.

For the LP perspective, I take a third-party perspective that assesses your VC fund as if it were a product that a third-party, in this case the LP, would potentially buy. This perspective is included to help you understand how LPs may assess you based on the decisions you make or, in some cases, don't make, related to the various components of setting up a fund. LPs, especially institutional LPs, like to think in terms of risk management – in this case a term meaning how risky or not risky a certain part of your operation may be. LPs often look for reasons to say no to investing in a fund; this book aims to help reduce your operational risk and help you set up a strong foundation on which to build your venture capital business.

THE FRAMEWORK OF THIS BOOK

UNDERSTAND THE THREE PHASES OF SETTING UP A VC FUND, THE CORE FUNCTIONAL AREAS NEEDED, AND HOW THEY ALL FIT TOGETHER

THE THREE PHASES OF SETTING UP A VC FUND

The functional areas are divided into three phases:

- Phase 1: Setting up the basics
- Phase 2: Setting up core functions as a venture capital fund
- Phase 3: Additional functions that will help prepare you to become an institutional firm

THE CORE FUNCTIONAL AREAS COVERED IN THIS BOOK

Unit 0. Basic legal, banking, and finance

Unit 1. Cloud provider

Unit 2. Telecommunications

Unit 3. Customer relationship management (CRM) system

Unit 4. Investor relations: marketing and sales

Unit 5. Legal

Unit 6. Bank

Unit 7. Fund administration, including valuations, accounting and bookkeeping

Unit 8. Tax

Unit 9. Additional functions expected by Institutional Limited Partners

Unit 10. Other concepts to consider when setting up a venture capital fund

HOW DO THE CORE FUNCTIONAL AREAS FIT INTO THE THREE PHASES OF SETTING UP A VC FUND

The functional areas for setting up a fund are presented in three phases. These phases build on each other, so the first phase is the most essential.

Phase 1: Setting up the basics

- **Unit 0. Basic legal, banking, and finance**
- **Unit 1. Cloud provider**
- **Unit 2. Telecommunications**
- **Unit 3. Customer relationship management (CRM) system**
- **Unit 4. Investor relations: marketing and sales**

Phase 1, setting up the basics, consists of five units. Big picture, this phase focuses on setting up the sales function for your new business known as your VC firm. It is important to set up everything in this phase before beginning to raise money for your venture capital fund.

Unit 0 starts with the basic legal, banking, and finance functions. The first step is to register your business. Keep it simple! Once you set up your business legally, you can use those legal documents, specifically your tax employer identification number (EIN), to open a bank account and credit card account for expenses. You'll then have to think about managing these accounts, which we will call finance.

Unit 1 covers choosing and setting up your cloud provider, which includes your file system, calendar, and e-mail. Typically this is either Google or Microsoft for business.

Unit 2 explores how to select and set up your telecommunications system, which is effectively setting up your means of communications, such as phones, teleconferencing tools, and the method you will use for cross-company communications (which may just be e-mail to start).

Unit 3 focuses on your customer relationship management system, which can essentially be thought of as the core database for all the relationships you will have at your venture capital firm. In practice, the CRM is usually a third-party software, though people also can run it from any spreadsheet. If you elect to use a spreadsheet, be aware that as you scale, running your business from a spreadsheet may become increasingly difficult.

Unit 4 involves the system you want to use to let people know you exist and to attract investors; it should include marketing, sales, and building brand.

Phase 1 is the foundational layer of setting up your venture capital firm. Once set up, you will be organized in a way that is scalable and that allows you to get your business off the ground. Phase 1 should be the most inexpensive phase and can be viewed as the earliest stage of business development while you learn if investors want to invest in your fund. If Phase 1 were summarized into a single piece of advice, it would be: (1) set up a means to communicate with prospective investors; (2) set up a way to track the people – in this case LPs – you are meeting so you can move them through a sales pipeline; and (3) make sure you have a system in place to let people know you exist!

Phase 2: Setting up your core function as a venture capital fund

- **Unit 5. Legal**

- **Unit 6. Bank**
- **Unit 7. Fund administration**
- **Unit 8. Tax**

Phase 2 focuses on setting up the core operations of your investment business once you confirm that you have investors.

Unit 5 covers preparing your legal foundation, which is effectively identifying and hiring a law firm to help you set up your firm and fund.

Unit 6 walks you through selecting a bank and setting up bank accounts for the firm and fund.

Unit 7 discusses finding and hiring a fund administrator, which will typically help you with valuation, accounting, and bookkeeping for your firm and fund.

Unit 8 offers ideas on choosing a tax firm, which will help you stay compliant with taxes, which cannot be escaped!

Phase 2 is a recommendation for the bare-bones version of running your venture capital fund. There is no venture capital fund without these core functions and service providers. Theoretically, you could simplify by having a fund contract in place with your investors (legal function) and a bank account for them to wire money into (bank function), while you handle the fund administration and tax filings, but practically this does not make sense. Nor is it recommended to take on too many operational functions yourself, especially considering that your core functions as a venture capital fund manager are investing and fundraising (and, depending on your strategy, also adding value to your portfolio companies). Setting up a VC fund is important, and something you will end up delegating, so think about the endgame from the start and avoid cutting corners. This is especially true if you want to raise institutional capital by getting investors from institutional LPs. They will hold you to a much higher standard of operations and risk management.

Phase 3: Setting up additional functions on your path to becoming an institutional firm

- **Unit 9. Additional functions expected by Institutional Limited Partners**
- **Unit 10. Other considerations when setting up your venture capital fund**

Phase 3 includes more advanced functional areas that will become increasingly important as you scale the business and the expectations of your investors increase. In Phase 3 you will lay the path to becoming more institutional. This means your compliance obligations will increase, as will your transparency requirements, and you will have to think about managing your risk more consistently. To manage these tasks, your team will have to scale commensurately with these increased responsibilities. As a reminder, this phase includes recommendations beyond the core functions introduced. You could adopt some functions from Phase 3 during Phase 1 and/or Phase 2. Think about starting with the end in mind, so that as your venture capital fund scales, you could implement any or all of these core functions.

PHASE 1: SETTING UP THE BASIC FUNCTIONS REQUIRED FOR YOUR VENTURE CAPITAL FIRM

In the beginning of this book, we defined the difference between the venture capital firm and the venture capital fund. The venture capital firm is the operating business that manages the fund. Phase 1 is only about setting up the venture capital firm and about managing personal risk, as well as wisely managing your time and money. Do not spend more money than you need at any point when setting up a venture capital fund. Think about this process of setting up a venture capital fund as a series of steps – across these steps you are looking to improve your chances of success. If you tried to do all of these steps at once, you would end up mismanaging the process. For example, some VC funds have cost hundreds of thousands of dollars to launch, with legal bills and employee salaries as the two biggest expenses. In the beginning, without compromising your chances of success, Phase 1, setting up the sales process, could cost less than $1,000.

UNIT 0. BASIC LEGAL, BANKING, AND FINANCE

The first step is to create a new business. In the beginning, it won't be called a management company; you are simply setting up a standard operating business. For the simple process of registering your business, use an online service, which should cost a few hundred dollars. In the U.S., you will set up an operating business, usually a limited liability company (LLC), and often in Delaware. This LLC becomes your management company after the fund is raised. Once your LLC is ready, you can use those official legal documents to open bank and credit card accounts for cash deposits and expenses. These three steps — setting up the LLC, setting up your bank account, and setting up your credit card account — help keep everything legally separate from your personal finances. It also simplifies accounting and tax requirements at the end of the year. In Phase 2, we will go into setting up legal and banking for the fund, but it is not necessary to set those up before the fund launches.

UNIT 1. CLOUD PROVIDER

WHAT IT IS, WHY YOU SHOULD HAVE IT, WHEN AND HOW YOU SHOULD IMPLEMENT IT, WHO SETS IT UP, AND WHETHER AN IT CONSULTANT SHOULD BE CONSIDERED

WHAT IS A CLOUD PROVIDER?

The cloud provider is the foundational layer of your firm. It's the equivalent of turning the lights on in the room or starting your computer. A cloud provider is a broad term for the internet-based technology company that provides the software system you will use to operate your venture capital firm. It is a third party that provides you with e-mail, cloud computing, and collaboration and productivity tools such as a file management system for organizing your business.

To keep things simple, the key tools you will first want to set up include a drive to store and organize your files, a calendar, and your email service. Since you are just getting started, it makes sense to go with the basics that will allow you to move forward with your fundraising process and get the fund off the ground. As you grow, you will have more budget to hire additional people, build more sophisticated business processes, and purchase additional software that can improve your firm. At first, though, the goal is to run as lean as possible to test the hypothesis for your fund and determine whether you can launch.

Let's start with the drive. Do not overthink it; this is a place to store your digital files and folders. Try to keep it as simple as possible at first, understanding that what you build now will ultimately change over time as you scale.

For your calendar, select an application that will allow you to quickly and easily set up meetings on both your computer and mobile phone, since you may be making appointments on the run in the beginning as you fundraise.

Your email service should be set up with an inbox specifically dedicated to the investment business. Keep in mind that as you scale your email may be read by a compliance officer, and your correspondence may be subject to inspection by one or more regulatory bodies that govern investment firms. Many VCs elect to use their personal email during this initial phase, an approach I don't recommend. This entire process of setting your firm up with a cloud provider should cost no more than $500.

WHY IS A CLOUD PROVIDER NECESSARY?

This is the software you will use every day to run your business. It provides an ecosystem of business tools from the start and will become the backbone of your firm's operations.

WHEN SHOULD A CLOUD TECHNOLOGY PROVIDER BE IMPLEMENTED?

A cloud provider is a priority for your business, and setting it up should be one of the first things you do. Again, some people do choose to use their personal accounts at first to conduct business.

HOW IS A CLOUD TECHNOLOGY PROVIDER INTEGRATED?

When choosing a cloud provider, consider the business applications that you will need for many of the necessary functions of your business, such as communications, content development, file management, and file storage. For example, provider Google Workspace offers Gmail, Google Drive, Google Docs, Google Sheets, Google Slides, Google Calendar, and more. Cloud provider Microsoft 365 includes Microsoft Outlook email, OneDrive, Microsoft Office, and other Microsoft business applications. While the success of your business will not hinge on this decision, do choose a product that you find comfortable and easy to use. It is generally a straightforward process to purchase what you need online with a credit card.

WHO IS RESPONSIBLE FOR SETTING UP A CLOUD PROVIDER?

You are! The founder or founders of the venture capital firm are responsible for setting up the cloud provider.

ADDITIONAL CONSIDERATIONS

Is an IT consultant necessary?

Getting a software system in place for your business could set you up for IT challenges, such as on-going management and maintenance and security issues. Should an IT consultant be hired to free you up to focus on investing? The answer is most likely no. It's unnecessary from a time and cost perspective. Day-to-day operations should not require much technical help, and while it may be required later on as part of your IT strategy, simply getting your business drive, calendar, and email up and running is initially enough.

UNIT 2. TELECOMMUNICATIONS

IMPLEMENTING TELECOMMUNICATIONS AND WHO IS RESPONSIBLE FOR SETTING IT UP

WHAT IS INCLUDED IN THE TERM TELECOMMUNICATIONS?

Telecommunications is a fancy word for the systems you set up for business communications. It includes your physical telephone(s), any accompanying phone plans, choosing and setting up a teleconferencing system such as Microsoft Teams, Google Meet, or Zoom, and the email system you've selected from your cloud provider.

WHY ARE TELECOMMUNICATIONS IMPORTANT?

In investing, two key advantages are information and time. Much depends on gathering more information, quickly. While running a venture capital firm is not the same as high speed trading per se, it does require consistent communication between founders, investors, and members of your team. Making sure you are set up to communicate smoothly with all necessary constituents will make your business run more smoothly.

WHEN SHOULD YOU IMPLEMENT TELECOMMUNICATIONS?

Setting up the foundation for business communications should be a priority at the beginning of this business venture. If you own a cell phone and have a phone plan, then you already have a way to connect with LPs, VCs, and founders. You may start your firm-building journey using your personal phone, but at some point you should set up a business phone or have your broader telecommunications strategy fall under your business' operating expenses.

HOW SHOULD A TELECOMMUNICATIONS SYSTEM BE IMPLEMENTED?

Basically, you should own a phone and have it on a data plan. If you are investing internationally, you should consider how you can communicate cost-effectively with international counterparts. A teleconferencing system is largely a matter of preference. You might choose one based on your cloud provider, i.e. how Google Meet works with Google Suite, or based on a teleconferencing software product you prefer. Consider the features that you will need. For example, if you plan to screenshare presentations, your teleconferencing system should include this feature. Other products you might consider for your firm's telecommunications include text, private messaging, or video tools.

WHO IS RESPONSIBLE FOR SETTING UP THE TELECOMMUNICATIONS SYSTEM?

You will set up your telecommunications.

ADDITIONAL CONSIDERATIONS

Should you hire an IT consultant?

IT challenges and security issues can always surface without warning. Do you need to hire an IT consultant? Only you can answer that question based on your technical skills, but most likely at this early stage you can troubleshoot most issues. As you scale, however, you may want to think about how telecommunications fit into your overall strategy. Because you will be operating a financial services business and there could be scrutiny of your communications at some point, hiring an internal or external IT professional can be prudent to help with new hires, compliance, and managing security.

UNIT 3. THE CUSTOMER RELATIONSHIP MANAGEMENT SYSTEM

LEARN WHAT GOES INTO CREATING A VERY GOOD CRM SYSTEM AND HOW TO BEST USE IT TO YOUR ADVANTAGE

WHAT IS A CUSTOMER RELATIONSHIP MANAGEMENT SYSTEM?

A Customer Relationship Management system is a broad term that refers to a business process used to track customers. Organizing data is the core of building a great CRM system. Without it the entire fundraising process is inefficient and ineffective. Some thought must go into how you will set up this system. Semi- and fully-customizable CRM software for sales teams is available and can be adapted for your own fundraising process. If you are trying to be frugal, you can also use any free spreadsheet software to organize and track your data, though spreadsheets can quickly become large, unwieldy, and difficult to update after only a few months. If the goal is a long-term business, you might opt for a CRM system that is designed to scale. In the context of a venture capital fund, the initial data you enter into your CRM will include potential Limited Partners. Over time, you will also use the CRM to track prospective investments, service providers, experts, and other individuals and companies relevant to your firm.

WHY IS A CRM SYSTEM NEEDED?

As mentioned above, the key reason to have a CRM system is to *organize your data* – you need to be organized in order to scale. A CRM system allows you to organize your network, track your interactions within that network, and understand how your network can best support the goals of your venture capital firm. Relationships are at the core of sales, and the CRM helps you track your relationships. Some VCs, when raising their first fund, will interact with as many as 1,000 prospective LPs. Without a CRM, or if you do not track your interactions with these potential investors in an organized way, you may lose sight of who is relevant to your business. You also may not be able to move them efficiently through a process. Your CRM should help you easily access information and answer questions such as: Who is ready for a second meeting? What did LP #391 want as a follow-up? Which company did LP #613 ask for clarifications on? Who do I need to send the fund's closing documents to? Which investors do I need to report to in order to stay compliant with my Limited Partnership Agreement (LPA)? A CRM system should be able to retrieve the data you need to answer all of these questions.

WHEN SHOULD YOU IMPLEMENT THE CRM?

The CRM should ideally be implemented when you first launch your venture capital firm. It will be a busy time, filled with discussions with service providers, prospective investors, and founders of start-ups. If you do not set up your CRM in the early days, you can quickly lose track of contacts, who you have already spoken with, what they want, necessary follow up, and where they could be integrated into your business in the future.

HOW SHOULD A CRM SYSTEM BE IMPLEMENTED?

There are many CRM software tools available to early-stage VCs. There are also CRM tools dedicated specifically to venture capital. Some VCs use CRM tools that are integrated directly into email. At a high level, you will use your CRM for multiple functions, including tracking LPs, service providers, companies you are considering investing in, and other people in your network. Consider carefully how interactions with these different customer types should be tracked. There will inevitably be some level of customization required to create a fully useful CRM. For example, if you are using your CRM to track LPs, then you may want a database able to track the LPs you have personally met with, those you've reached out to, and those you are going to meet with. After a meeting, you'll want to note in the CRM a variety of details about your discussion.

To reiterate, the best way to achieve results—which in the case of managing your LP network is to get them to invest into your fund—is to set up your CRM so that it's customized for the LP "sales funnel." It should be easy to use because you'll likely use it every day, multiple times per day, and it should help you achieve the results you define.

WHO IS RESPONSIBLE FOR SETTING UP A CRM SYSTEM?

You are responsible for setting up the CRM. As noted above, there is no need to set up a CRM from scratch. Rather, you can stand on the shoulders of VCs who have already set up CRMs that manage all the relationships you'll also want to track. If you have friends or connections who are VCs, they may be open to sharing their templates (even if they don't share the data in their CRM). You can get a head start in setting up your CRM using such templates. Once a CRM template is imported, you can continue to customize it for your specific business process needs.

ADDITIONAL CONSIDERATIONS

How can a CRM system offer a competitive advantage?

As a VC, managing your network well can create a competitive advantage, and a CRM exists to help you manage your network. For example, some LPs might invest in your fund if they believe you have a very strong network. Other VCs and founders might want to work with you because they believe your network can accelerate business growth. There are many ways that being able to organize and thereby readily make use of your network can give you a competitive advantage. Using your data to describe the value of your network just might help get LPs to invest in your fund over other funds or convince founders to take your capital. Hence the importance of the CRM.

When setting up your CRM, there are additional considerations, such as cost, ease-of-use, and how well the CRM integrates with other software and service providers you are already using or planning to use.

UNIT 4. INVESTOR RELATIONS: MARKETING AND SALES

INVESTOR RELATIONS IS AN ESSENTIAL FUNCTION FOR A VC AND SHOULD BE SET UP EARLY

Units 1-3 have been relatively straightforward. In Unit 1, you chose your cloud service provider, essentially turning the lights on in your business. In

Unit 2, you set up your communications system, so you are ready to begin your fundraising sales outreach process. In Unit 3, you set up your Customer Relationship Management system, allowing you to track your communications with prospective investors. In Unit 4 all of these pieces come together to support your sales process for fundraising.

WHAT DOES INVESTOR RELATIONS INVOLVE?

Investor relations describes the relationships you build with your investors where marketing and sales are at the core. The goal in marketing is to develop leads. The goal for sales is to find investors for your fund.

WHY ARE INVESTOR RELATIONS IMPORTANT?

A critical part of setting up a venture capital fund is creating the *function* of investor relations. Establishing respected and trusting relationships at the outset is invaluable, as fundraising is 100% a sales process. You must succeed at this level to progress to the next. Investor relations is therefore a core function of any venture capital fund.

WHEN SHOULD INVESTOR RELATIONS BEGIN?

The investor relations process should be well-planned from the earliest days of your venture. You'll want to carefully consider how you will communicate with prospective investors, track those conversations, and move the prospect through a sales process. Your goal is investors who will commit to and invest in your fund.

HOW ARE INVESTOR RELATIONS DEVELOPED?

Marketing and sales are the twin pillars of investor relations.

Generating leads for your sales pipeline requires marketing. Common marketing materials aimed at qualified prospective investors include a pitch deck or other proprietary content such as a white paper that dives deeper into insights you may have in a certain market. You might also develop a website—but be very careful with anything you put out into the public realm. There are many regulations and restrictions related to fundraising that must be adhered to. Also beware of leveraging your media and press connections to get an article written about you and your fundraising process. Best to consult with a lawyer before making any public fundraising announcements.

Your customer relationship management system is there to support your investor relations efforts to close the sale. Once you have prospective investors who are interested in your fund, make sure to answer their every question and provide any and all additional marketing materials they require for their investment decision. Refer to *How To Raise A Venture Capital Fund* for a comprehensive list of marketing materials that LPs may expect. When in doubt, ask the prospective LPs what additional information could help them finalize their investment decision.

WHO SHOULD BE RESPONSIBLE FOR INVESTOR RELATIONS?

In the beginning, you are responsible for investor relations. You will develop and execute your marketing plan and move prospective LPs through the sales pipeline. Managing those relationships in anticipation of the next fund is also important. In time, this role could be turned over to someone else. Near term, consider hiring support for your role as head of investor relations. This could be, for instance, an executive assistant who could help with prospecting, outreach, calendaring, CRM data management, and follow up.

ADDITIONAL CONSIDERATIONS

As a venture capitalist, you are seeking to invest in companies that you believe will increase in value and make your investors a profit. Investing is a very time-intensive business. You must identify and build relationships with founders, negotiate access into fundraising rounds of companies, and help those founders decide how to maximize new investment for growth. Investing in companies should be your priority, and you will consistently have to make trade-offs and prioritize how you spend your time.

When it comes to investor relations—which is a fulltime job on top of your job as investor— you should consider prioritizing relationships over marketing materials. Marketing materials, for example a pitch deck, can be outsourced. At least at the beginning, avoid outsourcing the relationship building you are doing with LPs. After all, you are asking them to give you significant amounts of capital. Putting yourself in their shoes, you would want to know and trust the person you are giving that check to, not someone who represents that person.

Keep in mind, as well, that you will always be developing your marketing materials. Everything is a working document that will need to be frequently revised as you continue to write, refine and share your materials. Aim for professional pieces, but give yourself the freedom to start your sales process as soon as possible. Do not get stuck in the rabbit hole. Find the balance between time spent refining your marketing materials and time invested in building relationships with prospective investors.

PHASE 2: SETTING UP THE BASIC FUNCTIONS OF YOUR VENTURE CAPITAL FUND

BASIC FUNCTIONS OF YOUR VC FUND AND THE CORE SERVICE PROVIDERS NEEDED TO RUN IT

By now it should be very clear that the venture capital firm is the operating business that manages the fund. In Phase 1, we explored how to set up the sales function in a cost-effective way without compromising the chances of success in raising your venture capital fund. Now it is time to layer in additional functions related to the fund itself – these include legal, banking, fund administration, and tax. These are the four essential pieces for launching a venture capital fund. Let's dive in!

UNIT 5. LEGAL CONSIDERATIONS RELATED TO A VC FIRM

WHAT IS THE LEGAL FUNCTION IN A VC FIRM AND FUND?

The legal function includes hiring a lawyer to draft the contract defining the relationship between you and your investors. This contract is called the Limited Partnership Agreement and Subscription Agreement.

WHY IS LEGAL SUPPORT NECESSARY?

Raising a fund involves many legal issues and you and your investor will need to work out a comprehensive legal agreement. You are operating within a regulated industry and you will need to manage liabilities. Legal assistance is prudent for your business to succeed.

WHEN IS A LEGAL TEAM ENGAGED?

There are two answers to this question.

First, you will want to hire a lawyer as early as possible in your fundraising process. Specifically, they will help you draft your initial terms, called a summary of terms. The summary of terms, usually two to 10 pages long, sets the basis for a discussion on the terms of the Limited Partnership Agreement, the contract between you and your investors. Hiring a lawyer early on may also help you stay compliant within the regulatory frameworks, which are subject to change. Legal support can be expensive; you'll want to time your needs accordingly. If your fund is not ready, you may have spent a lot of money with no recourse to pay it back. Therefore, use your legal support sparingly until you have more confidence that your fund will be raised.

When you are certain you are ready to hold a first close on your fund, this is the stage to turn to your legal team to help you draft your Limited Partnership Agreement and Subscription Agreements. The initial summary of terms will be expanded into your LPA. This can be a 100-200 page legal document and can cost between $50,000 and $250,000, or even more, using a standard law firm. If your strategy is complex and you end up negotiating many different terms with a variety of investors, your legal costs could rise.

HOW IS LEGAL SUPPORT ENGAGED FOR A VENTURE CAPITAL FIRM?

First, find a lawyer that focuses on fund formation. Get recommendations from experienced VCs and ask for an introduction. Interview several lawyers before making a decision, and choose the best fit for what you are building. Again, you will want to seek out lawyers who know both fund formation *and* venture capital. If their practice focuses primarily on just fund formation, they may work with hedge funds and may not have expertise in the nuances of venture capital. Alternatively, if they just know venture capital, they may be great at direct deals but may not understand the nuances of fund formation. Additionally, you may have specific needs based on your fund size, your fund strategy, and your geography, so be sure to spend some time qualifying your law firm before hiring them. When you are ready to move forward with a lawyer, their firm will conduct a check for any conflicts of interest and then prepare an engagement letter. Once you've signed this, the law firm can represent you in legal matters.

WHO SHOULD BE PART OF YOUR VC FIRM'S LEGAL TEAM?

At first, the legal team will be you and your lawyer. They will provide their legal perspective on terms, and their associates will draft the documents. This holds true for any additional side letter agreements you will have with LPs. Side letter agreements are terms you agree to in addition to the terms in the LPA.

ADDITIONAL CONSIDERATIONS

Firm versus fund perspective for the legal function

You will need separate legal support for the firm and the fund. Your lawyers are there to answer questions related to the operation of your firm. One example might be a question involving an employee contract. All legal expenses related to the firm are borne by the firm, not the fund. The fund's lawyer will, in turn, draft legal agreements for the fund. Expenses related to the fund are borne by the fund; that is, the fund will reimburse the firm for these expenses. Exactly which expenses are the fund's responsibility will be defined in the LPA. It is very important to properly track expenses between the firm and the fund.

What is the process for legally setting up a venture capital fund?

The legal entity for the operating business, called the venture capital firm, was introduced in Phase 1. The venture capital fund requires additional legal entities. In the U.S., this includes legally establishing the management company and at least two additional entities. Once negotiations with LPs have been finalized and they are ready to invest in your fund, they must fill out and sign two key documents. These are the Subscription Agreement and the Limited Partnership Agreement. The Subscription Agreement is the LP's application to subscribe to your fund. In it they must disclose information that allows you to make a decision about whether they legally can invest into your fund. This document also includes the amount they will invest. They sign this document first, and you countersign. This transaction accepts them into the fund. The LPA is the contract between you and the LP. It is signed by the LP to acknowledge the terms of the contract and countersigned by you to acknowledge an understanding of the terms of the contract.

How can a legal team be leveraged?

Law firms are there to provide legal advice, not business advice. Do not rely on your lawyer for input on how to run your business. Sure, you can listen to their perspective on what has worked for other clients, but ultimately you should develop the confidence to determine the best decisions for your business. Only rely on lawyers to draft legal documents that protect you. Your lawyer argues on your behalf only—not your investors'. A lawyer might offer a creative solution or advice, for instance, on how to structure something. It is wise to also seek opinions from other business colleagues.

What else could be considered when setting up the legal function?

Setting up legal entities can get complicated. Make sure to consult with your lawyer about optimizing for liability—basically, protecting you. This can involve your personal and tax liability and might extend to tax liability protection for your LPs. For example, if you accept capital from an institution, you'll want to make sure you won't jeopardize their tax-exempt status through something you do at your business. With international investments, make sure you are properly structured to take their capital without creating additional tax filing burdens for your LPs. Consult your lawyer case-by-case for specific issues that arise.

Your management company and part of your fund will have an operating agreement. These agreements should be drafted by your lawyer.

Certain filings could be handled by your lawyer, such as filing to get your employer identification number. This is needed to open a business bank account, to file taxes, and for other regulatory filings, such as the Form ADV in the U.S. Always consult your lawyer to be sure you understand your responsibilities.

Also consider having a law firm draft disclaimers for your pitch deck.

Questions should you ask your legal team before signing the engagement letter:

- How many VC funds of our size have you formed over the past two years?
- How many of those have had institutional investors?

- On what issues do you find institutions pushing back most? Where do they tend to negotiate hardest?

- Do you have an example of a difficult side letter negotiation and how you helped the VC get a favorable result?

- How do we know which terms are industry standard and which are not?

- Can you provide a list of the key terms most often negotiated and give us a sense for what is standard versus aggressive (for the General Partner (GP))?

- Do we need a private placement memorandum (PPM)? Why or why not?

- What are your thoughts on management fee waiver (cashless contribution) for the GP commitment?

- What expenses/expense categories can be billed against the Fund (LP) entity and what cannot?

- Fees for formation? Fees including side letters? Hourly fees for partner, associate, paralegal?

- Who will be our primary contact after we engage? Could we please speak with that person now?

- Timeline to create the formation documents, with and without a PPM?

- Do you have contacts in the LP community that may have an interest in this fund? If so, are you willing to circulate our materials and make introductions?

- Can you give us an estimate of how much it will cost to review the credit line documents (from specific banks that I may or will be working with)? Have you reviewed similar documents from these providers before?

- What, if any, mistakes have you seen VCs of our size and scale make with the LPA, formation, or raise process?

- Other attorneys have suggested that they will refrain from billing until we reach a first close. Is that something that can work for you?

Other questions to consider before hiring a law firm

- What is the engagement timeline?

- How difficult is it to switch law firms once you make the decision on the first fund?

- What are the implications of hiring the wrong firm?

- What will LPs think about the firm you have chosen to work with as counsel?

- Does a law firm bring any collaborations that could potentially reduce your expenses, such as a fund administrator that offers standardized documentation or a software company that simplifies the collection of documents and signatures for the fund closing process?

UNIT 6. THE WHO, WHAT, WHY, WHEN, AND HOW OF VC FUNDS AND BANKING

In Phase 1, you set up a bank account as part of the firm operating business to manage business expenses until the fund is raised. In Phase 2, you've hired a law firm to file the necessary forms for tax ID numbers, also referred to as employee identification numbers "(EINs)" for your fund's legal entities. The EINs, along with supporting documentation, will allow you to apply for bank accounts for the fund.

WHAT IS THE ROLE OF BANKING WHEN SETTING UP A VENTURE CAPITAL FUND?

Banking is a system. For the venture capital fund, a bank account is tied to a specific legal entity. This is a key point because the capital belongs to the investors in your fund – it does not belong to you. Therefore, you cannot commingle funds across entities. Banking is one of the simplest functions to understand – it's where your cash is held. It is also one of the most important functions to respect. If you do not set up the proper controls and manage cash appropriately by the rules, you stand to get into trouble. Best practices dictate that at least two people should always be required to sign off on any transfer of capital.

WHY IS BANKING A KEY PART OF SETTING UP A FUND?

You set up the banking function and consequent banking relationships in order to pay expenses, make investments, and generally manage the inflows and outflows of your firm and its funds.

WHEN SHOULD A BANKING SYSTEM BE SET UP?

A bank account is one of the first steps in setting up a venture capital fund. Every time you raise a fund, you will set up one or more bank accounts associated with that fund. If you raise a special purpose vehicle (SPV) in addition to your VC fund, you will need to add another bank account for each SPV.

HOW IS A BANKING SYSTEM SET UP?

You'll be setting up several bank accounts. These include an account for your management company, one for your fund, and additional accounts for any other entities, including any special purpose vehicles you decide to raise. These bank accounts are often within the same bank, although you can use multiple banks. If using more than one bank, make sure you design a treasury management strategy with your accounting firm and fund administrator. This will help keep track of funds, set up the correct processes for cash controls—including avoiding inappropriate commingling of funds across different accounts—and will optimize cash flow for improved performance, including internal rates of return.

Be sure to conduct due diligence on any bank. Have a list of questions for the banks you are interviewing to help you decide which bank can best serve your needs. For example, you might ask whether a bank has relationships with other venture capital firms or whether it provides credit facilities, sometimes called credit lines, which can help you manage cash flows when deploying your capital into investments.

These questions can help you determine whether a bank will meet your needs:

- Have you worked with venture capital funds before – which ones?

- Have you worked directly with Fund Administrators – which ones?

- Will our Fund Administrator have access to the accounts for setting up wires?

- How large is your team that supports VC firms?

- Will we have a dedicated contact person or team? Who is that person and can we connect now?

- Do you offer credit facilities to VC funds for capital calls? What are the standard terms for fees and repayment?

- Do you offer credit facilities to portfolio companies?

- What terms are currently offered for credit facilities?

- What information would you need from my firm to start a credit facility?

- How long does it take to open a credit facility?

- Are you able to underwrite illiquid securities?

- Is there anything else I should be aware of when starting a credit facility with your company?

- What does the platform look like and is it easy to use?

- Are you able to demonstrate the platform?

- What are the platform's wiring capabilities?

- What external systems can the bank sync to?

- What cash management products – on and off balance sheet – do you offer?

- What types of fees should I expect, for example maintenance or wire fees?

- What promotions do you provide if we choose your institution as our provider?

- Do you provide partner loans - on what economic terms and time period?

- What are your cyber security protections?

- What is your approval process for releasing wires under $25K? Over $25K?

- What's your biggest advantage/differentiation vs. *insert other bank's name here*.
- What is the compliance process for setting up an account here?
- What is the timeline for setting up a new bank account?
- Are there any limits to the number of accounts that can be set up for additional funds or special purpose vehicles?

WHO SHOULD BE PART OF A VC'S BANKING TEAM?

You set up your bank accounts with your banker. Elect to work with someone who is knowledgeable about venture capital, since there are idiosyncrasies that need to be addressed, including Know Your Customer (KYC) controls on the bank's side.

UNIT 7. FUND ADMINISTRATION AND ITS PURPOSE

WHAT IS FUND ADMINISTRATION?

Fund administration is essentially the back-end management of a fund. It includes activities such as accounting, financial reporting, creating financial statements and capital accounts, calling capital for investments, assisting with cash controls, managing LP data, and generally supporting the financial reporting for the fund.

The fund administrator is an outside group that you hire to support the management company that is your firm, as well as any additional legal entities you set up and, most importantly, the portfolios of investments associated with your fund. The fund administrator manages your bookkeeping, accounting, and valuations work that supports the financial reporting to your LPs. This allows you more time to focus on investing, fundraising, and building relationships.

WHY IS A THIRD PARTY ADMINISTRATOR NEEDED FOR A FUND?

The convenience and reliability of third party fund administrators has allowed the venture capital industry to expand significantly over the last decade.

The fund administrator can simplify the management of your fund and free you up to focus on other areas. For example, the fund administrator, with your permission and approval, can issue capital calls, handle quarterly accounting, manage distributions, and send out quarterly financial statements and capital accounts to LPs. They are not, however, considered a resource for purposes such as strategic business decisions.

WHEN DOES A VC ENGAGE WITH THE FUND ADMINISTRATOR?

There is no need to hire a fund administrator until after you have closed on capital for the fund and have signed legal agreements with LPs. However, you should prepare by interviewing potential fund administrators that could be a strong fit for your expected fund based on structure, strategy, and geography. Then, when you have a close on your fund, finalize the hiring of a fund administrator and utilize them to make the first capital call.

HOW IS FUND ADMINISTRATION SET UP?

Hiring an outside fund administrator means you don't need to set up these processes internally. You are hiring a third party service for their knowledge, expertise, and experience managing venture capital funds. Be sure to select a fund administrator that is deeply familiar with venture capital funds. Be transparent with your fund administrator. They will need to know your LPs, the size of their commitments to your fund, and all legal documents, including any side letters, so they can properly account for any financial terms.

WHO IS INCLUDED IN A FUND ADMINISTRATION TEAM?

In the beginning, you will be the leader of the fund administration team, in partnership with your fund administrator. There is usually one point of contact there that you will work with most closely and most likely a team supporting your account.

ADDITIONAL CONSIDERATIONS

Firm versus fund perspective for the fund administration function

Fund administration applies only to the fund. You hire a third party fund administration service provider with specific experience in administering funds and they are paid by the fund.

Questions to ask before hiring a fund administrator

- How many VC funds have you worked with of our size?

- Will we have a dedicated team and a point of contact? What is your team's tracked response time to email/phone calls?

- Who will be our primary point of contact after signing the engagement? Can we speak with that person now? How often do people in this role turn over?

- What are your fees for the GP, Fund, and Management Company entities? What are your expected price increases for these entities each year, if any?

- Will you provide a demonstration of your platform? Is there a dedicated GP portal and a separately dedicated LP portal?

- What features are provided by your platform? What metrics are tracked and reported to the firm and which are reported separately to the LPs?

- What access will LPs have to investment information and firm financials?

- When onboarding LPs, do you provide electronic documentation and signatures or do you use third party fund closing software?

- Do you provide tax services? What are the fees for these services?

- If you don't provide tax services, what tax providers do you most often work with? Who would you recommend for a fund of our size and scale?

- Explain your end of year accounting process and coordination with our tax provider.

What is the date by which K1s will be issued to our LPs?

- Can you walk through your product roadmap for the next year? What features and new capabilities should we expect?

- What is the biggest complaint that you hear from GPs that use your platform? And from LPs that use the platform?

- Have you worked with third-party audit firms to conduct an audit on a venture capital fund? If so, can you walk through the audit process?

UNIT 8. THE IMPORTANCE OF THE TAX FUNCTION

WHAT IS THE TAX FUNCTION?

The tax function is all about staying compliant with the governmental tax authority. It includes preparing for, filing, and potentially paying taxes for each year you run your firm and manage your fund.

WHY IS IT NECESSARY TO SET UP A SYSTEM FOR TAXES?

Taxes cannot be escaped. Taxes are required. Taxes are a permanent process every year. There are significant negative consequences to ignoring taxes. So treat this function as a critically important part of running a firm and managing a fund.

WHEN IS THE RIGHT TIME TO PREPARE FOR TAXES?

The rule of thumb is to always be preparing for taxes. As discussed in Phase 1, as soon as you set up bank and credit card accounts and start incurring expenses, you are responsible for tracking this information. This is called the finance function for your firm. Even though the fund administrator handles the accounting and financial statements of your fund, it is your responsibility to keep track of any and all documents that will be required by your fund administrator.

HOW IS THE TAX FUNCTION SET UP?

You will hire a third party tax firm to do your fund's taxes. Constant communication with your fund administrator is critical for accurate quarterly financial statements and capital accounts. Be sure to set up a drive, most likely via your cloud service provider, and save everything relevant here. When making a new investment, for example, save the final legal documents, and share this information with your fund administrator. This enables the administrator to update quarterly financial statements and year-end financial statements. These statements are then sent to the tax team to use to process tax documents such as the K1, a U.S. tax form that must be provided to investors in your fund. This tax team will also file the fund's taxes on your behalf, with your permission.

WHO SHOULD BE PART OF THE TAX TEAM? HOW IS THE TEAM SET UP?

As mentioned, your original tax team will include the third party tax service provider, the fund administrator, and you. One of your primary responsibilities is to save all of the investment files, including finalized legal documents and valuation support documents for your investments. Eventually, you might think about hiring more support on the finance and operations side and to help coordinate across the tax and fund administration functions.

ADDITIONAL CONSIDERATIONS

Firm versus fund perspective for the tax function

Both the firm and fund must pay taxes. For the firm, you will either file taxes yourself or hire a third party tax service provider. The firm pays for these services. You will also hire a third party tax service provider for the fund, and those expenses will be borne by the fund. In practice, the third party tax service provider could be the same for the firm and fund, or it could be two different providers.

Questions to ask before hiring a tax service provider

- What is your experience with GP fee waivers, i.e. cashless contributions to the fund?
- Have you worked with VC funds of our size? Do you generally review formation documents and do you provide recommendations for changes to the documents?
- Do you have a recommendation for a bookkeeper? Do you work with the

bookkeeper, i.e. noting appropriate fund expenses to track?

- What are your fees for each different legal entity? Do your fees change based on assets under management, number of investments, or number of LPs? If so, what are the price tiers?

- What expenses/expense categories can be billed against the fund entity and what cannot?

- Would we have a dedicated contact person and/or team? Who is that person and can we connect now?

- What is your end-of-year accounting process and how would you work with our fund administrator? What is the date by which K1s would be issued to our LPs?

- What challenges and differences in tax treatment should we expect for LPs domiciled internationally?

- What are some tax efficient strategies we should consider related to VC compensation?

- Are there any tax implications or considerations when recycling capital, for example, rolling early exit distributions back into the fund?

- How can you help us avoid running afoul of leveraged investments? As we utilize a credit line, for instance, at what point can we overstep and be considered a "leveraged investment" by an LP? Is there a ratio of capital raised or called versus the amount of the capital call line that has been lent that could put us at risk?

- If we are running SPVs, what is the preferred entity type?

- What are best practices for us to know with respect to Qualified Small Business Stock (QSBS)?

- What is the QSBS tax treatment for LPs that commit to the fund after we have made portfolio company investments?

- How would you treat a convertible and/or safe note as the issuance of a security?

- How do you recommend marking investments that have appreciated significantly but have not received a financing round in some time that reflects the increase in value?

- If applicable, would you work with funds incorporated outside of Delaware? If so, what issues should we be aware of?

PHASE 3: ADDITIONAL FUNCTIONS THAT SUPPORT GROWTH TO BECOMING AN INSTITUTIONAL FIRM

UNIT 9. FUNCTIONS EXPECTED BY INSTITUTIONAL LIMITED PARTNERS, INCLUDING THE AUDIT

UNDERSTANDING YOUR AUDIT

WHAT IS AN AUDIT?

An audit is a process conducted by a third party audit service provider that validates the financial compliance of a venture capital fund. Traditionally your fund administrator will prepare the financial statements of the fund, and your tax provider will assume these statements are correct and file the taxes. An auditor will provide a second opinion on the validity of the financial statements.

WHEN SHOULD AN AUDIT FIRM BE CONSIDERED?

An audit is considered an additional function in this book rather than a core function because many first-time and smaller funds are not required to get an audit. An audit is a fund expense. For a small fund, the percentage of that expense relative to the fund size is large. Since an audit is a second opinion and not absolutely required, as taxes are, VCs often prefer to forego it and instead use that budget to make additional investments for the portfolio. If you are lucky enough to have an institutional investor in your first fund, they will most likely require an audit. Having an institutional LP in your first fund suggests that you may be launching with a larger fund, so the audit expense in this case is relatively small.

Questions to ask before hiring an audit firm

As you begin to scale, and the cost of the audit as a percentage relative to the fund size decreases, you will most likely be required to get an audit to confirm your financial statements, including valuations and ownership.

Questions for a potential auditor are naturally very similar to those for a third party tax service provider:

- Is an audit required on a yearly basis? Does the size of the fund matter? What about year one?

- What is your experience with GP fee waivers i.e. cashless contributions to the fund?

- Have you worked with VC funds of our size? Do you review formation documents and provide recommendations for changes to these documents?

- What are your fees for different legal entities of the VC firm and fund? Do your fees change based on assets under management, number of investments, or number of LPs? If so, what are the price tiers?

- What expenses/expense categories can be billed against the fund entity and what cannot?

- Will we have a dedicated contact person and/or team? Who is that person and can we connect now?

- What is your end of year accounting process and how would you work with our fund administrator and tax provider?

- If we are running SPVs, do you also provide audit services for these?

- What are best practices with respect to QSBS?

- How are QSBS tax treatments handled for LPs that commit to the fund after we have made portfolio company investments?

- How would you treat each of a convertible and/or safe note as the issuance of a security?

- Have you ever had issues approving a venture fund's marks? If so, in what situation?

- How do you recommend marking investments that have appreciated significantly but have not received a financing round in some time that reflects the increase in value?

- If applicable, would you work with funds incorporated outside of Delaware? If so, what issues should we be aware of?

Firm versus fund perspective for the audit function

Audit applies only to the fund. The audit expense will be borne by the fund.

BUDGET

The budget is an important firm function as it relates to all expenses incurred by the firm. Similarly, the fund budget relates to all expenses borne by the fund. Managing the fund budget well will leave more capital to invest, and guarantee enough capital to cover future expenses and ensure the fund's survival. Your goal is to stay in business and avoid any personal liability for expenses at the fund level. Therefore, it is wise to find or create an initial budget and run through this careful exercise. As mentioned in Phase 1, you can start with a simple budget for the firm. Once the fund gets off the ground in Phase 2, you can build out the fund budget.

Firm versus fund perspective for the budget function

The budget applies to both the fund and firm. It is extremely important to know the difference between expenses related to the firm and those related to the fund. Incorrectly charging unrelated expenses to the fund can get you in trouble with your LPs and the regulatory bodies for investment funds.

INSURANCE

Insurance is a standard function. There are two core reasons for getting insurance – to manage your personal and your business' liability. At first, the major types of insurance for a new venture capital fund will be general liability, executive liability, workers' compensation, and cyber. A fund administrator may suggest how best to allocate the insurance expense across the firm and the fund.

Firm versus fund perspective for the insurance function

Insurance applies to the firm and the fund, though you will usually buy one consolidated policy. Again, make sure you triple-check how insurance expenses are allocated.

COMPLIANCE

Building out your compliance function should begin on Day 1. As you scale, the complexity of the firm and its various funds will increase. When setting up the firm and fund, consider compliance as nine categories: business, regulatory, Limited Partnership Agreement, fund, tax, firm policies, processes, IT, and valuation.

For business, you will be expected to maintain registrations each year your business exists. These can be federal and state level filings.

For regulatory, you will need to consult with your lawyers on all the different filings required, such as the Federal Form D filing, or various state-specific filings, such as Blue Sky filings. Compliance requirements can change year to year, so regular monitoring is necessary.

The LPA is a signed contract with your investors which governs the fund. Stay compliant with the terms in this contract. Your law firm and fund administrator can help with this category, but ultimately you are responsible for staying compliant with your LPA. Should you ever need to change this contract, you will have to amend the LPA with the approval of your LPs. An approved amendment is the only way to change this contract once signed.

For the fund, similar to business, you will have to maintain certain filings each year. This could be consolidated with regulatory compliance.

Tax compliance involves meeting proper filing deadlines.

You would most likely consult a third party compliance firm to help you draft certain firm policies. These policies exist to help put you in a stronger position to raise institutional capital. Examples might include a privacy policy, insider trader policy, anti-bribery and corruption policy, anti-money laundering/know your customer policy, and political contributions policy. Institutional investors will expect you to have and maintain compliance with such policies.

Processes is a general category that indicates compliance with certain policies that are *non-negotiable* for many LPs. For example, this could include a dual signature process to release wire transfers from the fund. Setting up and complying with sound business policies negates the risk of mismanaging your business or injuring your chances of securing institutional capital.

Information Technology (IT) security refers to setting up a firewall and managing the protection of your and all your employees' data and mobile devices. It is especially important when traveling and because so much work is done directly from mobile phones.

Valuation refers to staying compliant with your valuation policy, which may be drafted in coordination with your fund administrator. They, and an auditor if you elect to have one, can help you stay compliant.

Firm versus fund perspective for the compliance function

Compliance applies to the firm and fund.

INFORMATION TECHNOLOGY

Information Technology is its own function and is all about managing the IT infrastructure of your firm. It can mean IT security, as mentioned above in compliance. It can also refer to who will solve any IT challenges that arise in the daily running of your firm, such as protecting proprietary data, including having back-ups of that data for business continuity and disaster recovery. IT can mean password protection. It can refer to protecting your bank account information and any financial information related to your finances. As your firm begins to scale, you may want to hire a third party IT service provider who can draft an IT policy for your firm and help you manage the many aspects of your firm's IT security and infrastructure.

Firm versus fund perspective for the IT function

IT applies to the firm and fund and refers to protecting your data, including LP data for the fund. Make sure to understand the implications of misusing personally identifiable information.

HUMAN RELATIONS

Human relations is the function of managing employees as your firm scales. HR software can make it easy to set up payroll, manage tax withholdings, employee benefits, and other issues related to your firm.

Firm versus fund perspective for the human relations function

HR applies only to the firm. While the firm manages the fund, HR is a firm expense, and it is managed at the firm level.

OFFICE SPACE

Office space can be a function at some point. Though not necessary before raising a fund, having your own space can have its benefits. When possible, build this into your budget and account for a physical space to run your sales process for Phase 1 and beyond. The details of this function can include finding space, negotiating the lease, lease renewal, meeting the lease payments, and potentially some additional management obligations that come with being in a physical space.

Firm versus fund perspective for the office space function

Office space applies only to the firm.

UNIT 10. OTHER CONSIDERATIONS WHEN SETTING UP YOUR VENTURE CAPITAL FUND

FIRM VERSUS FUND PERSPECTIVE: YOU ARE RUNNING TWO BUSINESSES!

The many things involved in setting up a venture capital fund can be confusing. You are not just setting up one business. Rather, you are setting up two businesses: the firm and the fund.

To recap: the firm, or management company, is the operating business that you set up and manage. It pays for salaries, employee benefits, rent, and other expenses, such as software used to run business processes of the firm. The firm will also have its own accounting, tax, legal, insurance, and marketing expenses. These will be separate from the fund expenses for these same functions. Keep them separate. Consult a lawyer or fund administrator if you need to confirm what your LPA says about expense allocation.

The fund, as we have outlined above, is the legal entity you set up to house the portfolio of investments. The fund is obviously managed in conjunction with the firm, but it has its own budget, processes, systems, software, and service providers. The fund pays for expenses that are relevant to the management of the fund. This means that you are not paying for it personally; rather, your fund investors are paying for it. Respect this dynamic! Keep in mind that every dollar you spend via the fund is a dollar that is not available to invest in a 100x company, so spend wisely. Expenses that are typically borne by the fund include: fund administration, including accounting for the fund; valuations; tax; audit; legal, including organizational expenses; interest on lines of credit; insurance; and any other expenses defined in your fund's LPA.

Looking back at Phase 1, we walked through the steps of setting up the firm. It is fairly simple to set up a new business entity and a few functions that will support you in the other, larger process of raising a fund. Phase 1 can practically be run in conjunction with my other book *How To Raise A Venture Capital Fund*.

Once a successful fund is raised, you'll then add in the additional functions from Phase 2 and Phase 3, which are required to manage the fund.

MANAGING TWO FUND CUSTOMERS: THE FOUNDER AND THE LP

Venture capital is centered on relationships. When setting up a venture capital fund, you are setting up a business to serve two core customers: the founder and the LP. You must manage these relationships, and the data behind these relationships, separately.

The founder is the person or team you will invest in. These are people with a company or an idea that you believe has significant growth potential. This may also be viewed as the "deal" or "investment" side of the venture capital fund. You will need to track founders and the companies they are running. These companies will, in turn, also have data that must be tracked. You will eventually have a pipeline for investments and work flows related to your personal investment and decision-making processes, but for the purposes of this book we haven't gone into how to set these up. But keep in mind that some of the decisions you make when setting up your fund, such as choosing your CRM, will have implications for how well you can manage the investment processes later on once the fund is off the ground. Look ahead and try to see the bigger picture as you make firm decisions. Ask yourself whether your business processes will be stronger or weaker in the future because of that decision.

The LP is the investor in your fund. The steps outlined in Phase 1, especially those for setting up the firm's CRM, were focused on creating a process and system to track your relationships with LPs.

THE PROCESS OF INSTITUTIONALIZING A VENTURE CAPITAL FUND

The information in this book is divided into three phases to save you money and time and to help you understand that setting up a venture capital fund should be viewed as an ongoing journey. Launching and building an investment firm is an iterative process.

I have recommended throughout this book that it is not necessary to implement everything at once. Part of being a fund manager is knowing the order of operations and being able to properly prioritize what is necessary now and what will be necessary in the future. Phase 1 is about setting up the business and specifically the sales function that will enable you to begin to raise a fund. Phase 2 focuses on implementing the essential functions for running a venture capital fund. Phase 3 outlines the additional functions that will be required as your business grows and you take on larger LPs, including institutions. Similar to how a public company will have different processes than a startup company, your first-time fund will have different processes than your firm 10 years from now. Be aware that expectations will increase, and processes will most likely have to change over time. This book provides the core concepts of setting up a venture capital fund and gives a peek into the future of what you can expect as you experience greater and greater success.

DEFINING AND MANAGING OPERATIONAL INFRASTRUCTURE

There is a key concept running through Phases 1, 2, and 3: iteration. The point is that expectations will increase as you scale your business. Meeting these enhanced expectations will require you to always run a better business. My best advice is to aim for every process to be best-in-class. Every system should ideally make you more productive and your workflows more efficient and well-coordinated across your organization, especially as you raise follow-on funds. The combination of these continual improvements will result in a constant leveling up of your firm. This may sound like a lot of pressure, especially for many of the operations that are independent from investing, fundraising, and adding value, but the end result is worth it.

As I see it, the core functions work in tandem. For example, to complete your fund's taxes, you will need to have a well-organized file management system and work effectively with your fund administrator to get the tax team the correct information. As you run your business processes, constantly think about the relationships between core functions and identify improvements that can help strengthen your firm.

At my firm, Coolwater, one function I especially focus on is the *Strategic CFO*. This is an effective financial and operational perspective. It ensures that finances are organized and accurate, that operations are well coordinated, transparent, and effective, and that everything is and stays in compliance.

This idea of defining and managing your operational infrastructure has a strategic lens, meaning it requires a perspective of constant improvement. Perhaps this concept is embodied in *kaizen*, the Japanese concept of continuous improvement. As you scale, this continuous improvement of your operational infrastructure will eventually have to be taken over by someone else, the Strategic CFO. They will likely have additional responsibilities such as cash management, portfolio construction, portfolio management and scenario planning, in addition to coordinating and executing ever-larger financial and operational tasks.

THE MODULARIZATION AND SPECIALIZATION OF SETTING UP A VENTURE CAPITAL FUND

This book describes the simplest way to set up a venture capital fund. It offers the essential steps needed to set up a firm, to raise a fund, and to prepare the operating infrastructure to manage a fund.

Keep in mind that there may be additional service providers and software tools that can make this process easier. The trade-off is usually between doing it manually and adopting a new system, which can be time-consuming and more costly. However, try to keep an open mind and consider each option. Below are two examples of how modularization and specialization of venture capital has enabled more venture capital funds to launch and be managed better.

Example one: Historically, a law firm would manage all of the processes related to closing the contracts with your investors. However, there is now software to help gather and organize the documents and then share this information efficiently with your lawyer and fund administrator. This software can save money that otherwise would be spent on lawyers whose core competency is not organizing documents and sending data.

Example two: You may have multiple banks and/or bank accounts. A new treasury management software comes out that would allow you to earn additional yield on this cash as it sits idle in the bank between investments. Usually, this is something you wouldn't think about, but it demonstrates that as the industry matures, there can be opportunities to leverage new services and software to the benefit of your fund. Take advantage of these opportunities as they arise.

Please reach out to me at winter@coolwatercap.com if you would like to learn more about ways to work together.

COMPENDIUM: KEY TAKE-AWAYS

By now you should be very familiar with the idea that setting up a venture capital fund means that you are setting up an operating business, the venture capital firm, and a venture capital fund, which is a legal entity between you and your investors, that invests in companies.

When setting up a venture capital fund, there are "core" functions that are essential from the start and "extra credit" functions that you will most likely have to implement over time, especially if you would like to involve Institutional Limited Partners. Please see my book *How To Raise A Venture Capital Fund* for more perspective on what is required to raise funds from ILPs.

EPILOGUE: WHAT THIS BOOK IS…
AND WHAT IT IS NOT

I wrote this book as a guide for fund managers who are embarking on the journey of setting up their first venture capital fund. While I have given thought to other funds in the alternatives markets – for example, private equity funds, hedge funds, and real estate funds – I deliberately chose to keep this book straightforward and simple for this particular audience.

The book offers one opinion on how to set up a venture capital fund. While this is not the only way, I have helped over 175 VC funds launch from scratch and along the way have developed an informed perspective on the core functions and evolution of this fund-building journey.

The focus here is solely on setting up a venture capital fund. My next guide will focus on how to manage the venture capital fund once you have it. How you manage your fund is key to achieving success. You'll want to make sure you are setting up the right business processes and systems to manage the fund effectively.

Interested in learning more about how to manage a venture capital fund? Please reach out to me. I look forward to hearing from you.

ABOUT THE AUTHOR

Winter Mead is the Founder and Managing Member of the investment firm Coolwater Capital, which exclusively focuses on emerging managers and technology investments. Coolwater is an academy for training, building and scaling emerging managers, a curated community of VC investors and early-stage investment specialists, and an investment firm. Coolwater has helped launch over 175 emerging managers, establishing strong ties and trust with these managers, who form the foundation of the Coolwater community. Winter is also the author of How To Raise A Venture Capital Fund. Prior to Coolwater, he played a key investor role in an evergreen investment fund at SAP, co-founded the LP transparency movement called #OpenLP, and served on the committee for the Institutional Limited Partners Association (ILPA), which sets the standards for the private equity industry. Winter's extensive experience includes private equity and venture capital roles in San Francisco, institutional fund investments, direct technology investments, and angel investing. He also served as junior faculty at Stanford Graduate School of Business, holds degrees from the University of Oxford and Harvard University, and now resides in Utah with his family, passionately solving business challenges.

www.ingramcontent.com/pod-product-compliance
Lightning Source LLC
LaVergne TN
LVHW010358070526
838199LV00065B/5854